# A HISTORICAL ALBUM OF
# MICHIGAN

*Front and back cover: "City of Detroit, Michigan." Painted by William James Bennett, 1837. Courtesy of the New York Public Library.*

*Title page: Michigan Woods at Christmas. Photograph by Amy Suhay.*

Library of Congress Cataloging-in-Publication Data

Wills, Charles.
    A historical album of Michigan / Charles A. Wills.
       p.    cm. — (Historical albums)
    Includes bibliographical references (p. 62) and index.
    Summary: Surveys the history of Michigan, from the time of its
first settlers through its industrial, political, and social development
to current economic and environmental concerns. Gazetteer includes
map, statistics, and other facts.
    ISBN 0-7613-0036-8 (lib. bdg.)   ISBN 0-7613-0126-7 (pbk.)
    1. Michigan—History—Juvenile literature. 2. Michigan—
Gazetteers—Juvenile literature. [1. Michigan—History]
I. Title. II. Series.
F566.3.W55.  1996
977.4—dc20                            96-16378
                                     CIP
                                     AC

 **Created in association with Media Projects Incorporated**

    C. Carter Smith, *Executive Editor*
    Douglas Hill, *Project Editor*
    Charles Wills, *Principal Writer*
    Bernard Schleifer, *Art Director*
    Christina Hamme, *Production Editor*
    Arlene Goldberg, *Cartographer*

    Consultant: Ken Hack, Concord Community Schools, Concord, Michigan

# CONTENTS

A HISTORICAL ALBUM OF

# MICHIGAN

Charles A. Wills

THE MILLBROOK PRESS, Brookfield, Connecticut

# Introduction

Among the states, Michigan's geography is unique, and this unique geography has shaped its history.

Although it lies far from any ocean, Michigan is surrounded by water. The state borders four of the five Great Lakes and is second only to Alaska in the length of its coastline. Michigan is the 23rd-largest state in land area, but if Michigan's water area were counted, it would be the largest state east of the Mississippi River!

The state is divided into two peninsulas—the Upper and Lower—separated by the Straits of Mackinac. Although the Upper Peninsula was the first to be explored in the 1600s, settlement began on the Lower Peninsula, and even today the vast majority of the state's people live in lower Michigan. The two peninsulas weren't even linked by a bridge until 1957.

The Great Lakes and the state's rivers provided a natural highway for the Native Americans who once roamed Michigan's woods and for the French missionaries and explorers who reached the region in the 1600s. But Michigan's watery geography could also be an obstacle: American settlement didn't really take off until the Erie Canal linked the Michigan Territory with New York and New England.

Closer to our own time, Michigan's waterways carried the iron ore and other raw materials for the state's car factories—factories that have forever linked Michigan, especially Detroit, with the automobile age.

Finally, Michigan's lakes, rivers, streams, and coves make the state a paradise for vacationers. Watch the sun rise over mighty Lake Huron, or cast for trout in a rushing stream, and you'll certainly agree with Michigan's motto— "If You Seek a Pleasant Peninsula, Look Around You."

# PART ONE

# THE LAND BESIDE THE LAKES

Statuesque lighthouses dot Michigan's thousand miles of Great Lakes shore. The Pointe Aux Barques lighthouse on the Lower Peninsula has guided ships across Lake Huron since 1857.

The two peninsulas that make up Michigan were home to several Native American cultures before the arrival of the first European explorers in the 1600s. French missionaries and traders established a presence in the region, but in the mid-1700s the British gained control. After the Revolutionary War, Michigan became part of the United States. Settlement began in earnest in the territorial years (1805–1837), as people from New England, New York State, and Europe arrived to establish farms and towns. Michigan attained statehood in 1837, and the 19th century saw the development of industries like mining and lumber.

# Early Michigan

In the distant past Michigan lay under a great inland ocean. Over time the waters fell back, creating dry land. The region's climate was much warmer then, and tropical forests covered the land. The remains of the plants and animals that lived in prehistoric Michigan decayed and became fossilized, creating great deposits of coal and iron ore.

About 10,000 years ago, vast rivers of ice called glaciers slowly pushed south from what is now Canada. The glaciers cut deeply into the earth and then melted, creating the five Great Lakes that lie in the center of North America. They also carved the Straits of Mackinac—the waterway that divides Michigan into two peninsulas, the Upper and Lower.

Like the ancient ocean, the glaciers, too, fell back over time. They left behind a land of gently rolling hills covered with forests of pine and hardwood trees, cut through by many streams and rivers, and dotted with lakes and ponds.

The first people arrived in Michigan a few thousand years after the retreat of the glaciers. Not much is known about these early Michiganders, but archaeologists (scientists who study ancient peoples) have discovered that they mined the Upper Peninsula's abundant deposits of copper, which they used to make tools.

A Native American smelts iron by heating ore-bearing rocks on the shores of Lake Superior. Archaeologists have found evidence that Michigan's ancient peoples fashioned copper tools as early as 3000 B.C., making them among the world's first metalworkers.

Later, Michigan became the northernmost outpost of the Mound Builders, the name given to a Native American civilization that developed to the south of the Great Lakes. Their name comes from the great earth mounds they built, probably for ceremonial purposes. A few mounds have been found within Michigan's borders, most near the city of Grand Rapids. By A.D. 1500—about the time European explorers began to reach the shores of North America—the Mound Builder culture had completely disappeared.

When the first Europeans finally reached Michigan about 150 years later, they found several Native American nations living in the region. The rugged forests of the Upper Peninsula were home to both the Chippewas (also called the Ojibways) and the Menominees. On the Lower Peninsula lived the Miamis, the Ottawas, and the Potawatomis. All these groups spoke versions of the Algonquian language, a language they shared with other Native American societies from Canada to the Carolinas. Michigan's name comes from *michi gama*, an Algonquian phrase meaning "great water."

Besides the Algonquian-speaking groups, the Detroit area was the territory of the Hurons, or Wyandots. Called the Hurons after the French word *huré* in reference to their bristly hairstyles, these people spoke an Iroquoian language. They probably

Michigan's Native Americans believed that powerful spirits lived all around them as parts of the natural world. The Ottawas, for example, worshiped a spirit called Nanabozho who lived in the sky above Mackinac Island. The Thunderbird, a phoenix-like spirit (shown here in an early pottery design), also appeared in the religion of many Great Lakes tribes.

had migrated to Michigan under pressure from the Iroquois, a powerful group of Native American nations that lived in New York State.

The Hurons lived in longhouses—long, round-roofed structures big enough to house several families. They built on high ground, near a river or a spring, and surrounded their villages with palisades (fences).

Michigan's Algonquian-speaking peoples shared a similar way of life. They lived in small villages, usually alongside streams or rivers. Families lived in wigwams—houses made of a framework of young trees and covered with sheets of bark.

Men hunted and fished; women tended crops of corn, beans, squash, sunflowers, and tobacco on patches of farmland cleared from the forest. *Sangamite*, a stew of cornmeal and meat or fish, was the staple food.

Michigan's Native Americans were great travelers and traders. Their birch-bark canoes were ideal for travel on Michigan's waterways. The craft were light enough to be carried short distances between rivers but sturdy enough for travel on the Great Lakes or across the Straits of Mackinac.

No one knows how many Native Americans lived in Michigan at the time of first contact with European explorers—perhaps as many as 100,000 or as few as 15,000. But only a few thousand remained in the region by the time it became an American state.

A French engraving from 1688 shows a Native American village in present-day Michigan surrounded by a palisade (fence) of logs for defense against attack. The longhouse-style dwellings shown here suggest this may have been a Huron village.

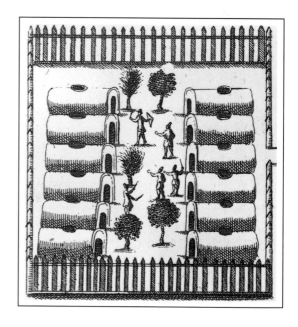

# Furs and Forts

Frenchmen were the first Europeans to set foot in Michigan. In 1618, ten years after he had founded the settlement of Quebec on the St. Lawrence River and claimed Canada for France, Samuel de Champlain sent a young man named Etienne Brulé on an exploring journey. Champlain hoped Brulé would find the Northwest Passage—a waterway believed to run through North America to the riches of Asia.

For several years Brulé and his companions searched for the legendary passage. Details of his voyage are sketchy, but at some point, probably in 1621, he passed through the Sault Sainte Marie—the rapids that separate Lake Huron from Lake Superior—and visited the Upper Peninsula.

A few years later, Champlain dispatched Jean Nicolet on a similar mission. Nicolet was so sure he would reach Asia that he packed a suit of silk robes to wear at the court of the Khan, or emperor, of China. Nicolet made it only as far west as present-day Green Bay, Wisconsin, where he greeted curious Native Americans in his Chinese costume. Along the way he passed through the Straits of Mackinac and explored the shores of Lake Michigan.

Neither explorer found the passage (it didn't exist) but they found some-

Explorer Samuel de Champlain (1567–1635) became governor of New France in 1612. Champlain was eager to extend France's North American territory from its base in Quebec, and under his leadership the first Frenchmen reached the region that became Michigan.

thing valuable in the land along the lakes: furs. The pelts of beavers and other animals fetched high prices in the markets of Europe. By 1650, scores of adventurous fur traders—mostly young Frenchmen or Canadians—were paddling down the St. Lawrence and onto the lakes to trade for furs with the Native American trappers.

These traders fell into two groups. The first, the *coureurs des bois* ("runners of the woods") journeyed on foot through the region's thick forests. The second group, the *voyageurs* (voyagers), paddled canoes along Michigan's rivers and streams.

Although the French wanted only to trade, not to settle permanently, their coming greatly changed life for the region's Native Americans. Many abandoned their crops and did little but hunt fur-bearing animals to trade with the French. Some became addicted to the brandy the French brought in return for beaver pelts. Others were killed by diseases, especially smallpox, which had been unknown before the French arrived.

*Voyageurs* **sometimes rigged sails to their birchbark canoes (top left), although they usually paddled their craft through Michigan's lakes.**

**The settlement at the Sault Sainte Marie (bottom left) as it looked around 1700, thirty years after its founding by Jacques Marquette. The dwellings along the shore housed many of the Chippewas and Ottawas who traded furs with the** *voyageurs.*

On the heels of the *coureurs des bois* and the *voyageurs* came missionaries, most of them priests of the Jesuit order, for the French wanted to convert the region's Native Americans to Christianity.

As early as 1641, two Jesuit priests, Charles Raymbault and Isaac Jogues, reached the rapids of Sault Sainte Marie. Just twenty-seven years later, the missionary Jacques Marquette established a mission (religious settlement) there. Historians consider this mission the first European settlement in Michigan.

**In this 19th-century engraving (below), a Jesuit missionary preaches to a group of Native Americans around a campfire. The Jesuits were required to send a detailed report to their superiors each year, and these are now a valuable source of knowledge about life in New France.**

These missionaries had great faith and courage. In fact, many were killed by Native Americans or died of hardship. Still, they made few converts.

As French influence continued to spread throughout the Great Lakes and south along the Mississippi River, a series of military outposts sprang up in Michigan. The first, on the Straits of Mackinac near present-day Mackinaw City, was built in the early 1670s. It eventually became known as Fort Michilimackinac.

Another great explorer, Robert Cavelier, Sieur de La Salle, built several outposts on the shores of Lake Michigan. La Salle also built the first ship to sail the Great Lakes, the *Griffon*. He hoped the *Griffon* would carry furs back to Canada, but it disappeared without a trace in November 1679.

In 1699, Antoine de la Mothe Cadillac, commandant (commander) at Fort Michilimackinac, decided another post was needed to the south. The English, who had colonized much of North America's east coast, were now arming the fierce Iroquois and urging them to make war against the French, and against the Hurons, France's chief Native American ally in lower Michigan.

To keep the Iroquois and English out of Michigan, Cadillac led 100 soldiers to the *place du detroit*—"the place of the strait" in French—and in 1701 a log fort rose along the shore. Later, *habitants* (settlers) arrived.

Robert Cavelier, Sieur de La Salle (1643-1687), built a fort on the site of present-day St. Joseph, Michigan, in 1679. La Salle's dream was to establish a string of French forts and settlements from the Great Lakes to the mouth of the Mississippi River.

# Four Flags Over Michigan

Detroit's growth was slow. A half-century after its founding, the settlement was home to just 650 people. There was a garrison of 100 soldiers, and the rest were mostly habitants who farmed plots along the Detroit River. A few hundred other soldiers, traders, missionaries, and settlers were scattered throughout Michigan.

By the mid-1700s, in fact, only about 50,000 people lived in New France—Canada and the French-claimed lands along the Great Lakes and in the Mississippi River Valley.

In contrast, the thirteen British colonies on the East Coast had a population of more than a million.

Britain and France had already fought several wars in North America by 1754, when another major conflict, the French and Indian War, broke out. It ended with France's defeat. In a peace treaty signed in 1763 France gave up practically all of its North American territory.

By the time the treaty was signed, Michigan was already under British

**This map of Detroit was printed in Paris in 1764. The habitations marked at the top are the farms of the settlers; the inset shows a plan of the fort that defended the small settlement.**

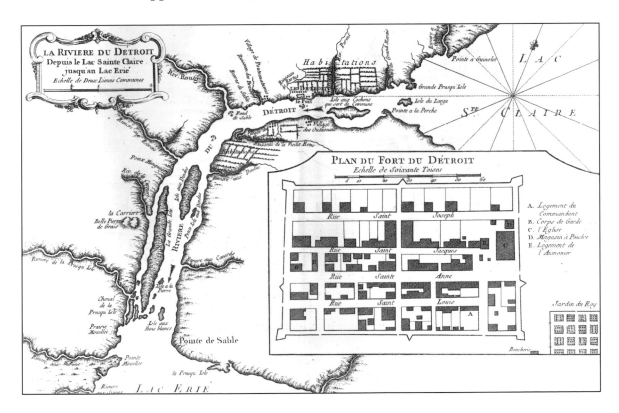

15

rule. On November 20, 1760, the garrison at Detroit had surrendered to Major Robert Rogers, leader of a band of colonial frontiersmen.

Michigan's French-speaking habitants accepted British rule peacefully. The region's Native Americans did not. The French had taken the trouble to treat the Native Americans well. The British, however, were more high-handed and less respectful in their dealings with Native Americans.

In the spring of 1763, Native American anger at Michigan's new rulers led to war.

Pontiac, an Ottawa chief, was enraged by Britain's failure to recognize him as a great ruler. He secretly organized an alliance of Native American groups from around the Great Lakes. His aim was to drive the British from their forts, including Detroit, by surprise attack.

On the morning of May 7, Pontiac and 300 warriors entered the fort at Detroit to meet with the British commander. The Native Americans carried sawed-off muskets under their robes. They never got the chance to use them: The British soldiers were standing warily with their own muskets at the ready. Someone—no one knows exactly who—had warned the British.

Pontiac rapidly assembled 900 warriors and surrounded the fort. Meanwhile, other Native American war parties seized or tried to seize British forts as far away as Pennsylvania and New York. Out of the fourteen forts attacked, they successfully managed to capture ten.

Detroit was able to hold off the Native Americans for nearly six months, until Pontiac's warriors gave up the siege. By that time the other forts which had fallen to the Native Americans had been recaptured, too. Although the British would later call the uprising Pontiac's Rebellion, in fact the Ottawa leader only planned the attack on Detroit and a few other forts around the Great Lakes.

Twelve years later the British faced another rebellion. This time it was the citizens of the thirteen colonies who rose up to demand independence as the United States of America.

Henry Hamilton, British commander at Detroit, sent pro-British Native Americans on raids into Pennsylvania and against Patriot (pro-independence) settlers along the Ohio River. Anger over the raids led a rugged frontiersman named George Rogers Clark to lead a small band of Patriots on a daring winter march into the Great Lakes region. Although Detroit remained in British hands, Clark seized other important British outposts and captured Hamilton at Vincennes in present-day Indiana.

After giving up the siege of Detroit, Pontiac traveled to Britain's Fort Pitt in Pennsylvania to surrender. Here he negotiates surrender terms with Colonel Henry Bouquet. Pontiac later traveled to what is now Illinois, where he was murdered by another Native American in 1769.

In 1781, Spain, which had entered the war on the Patriot side three years earlier, sent a small force of troops to Michigan from St. Louis in present-day Missouri. The Spanish briefly captured Fort St. Joseph, near what is now the town of Niles, before returning to St. Louis. Thus, the flags of four nations—France, Britain, Spain, and the United States—have flown over this corner of the state.

The United States won its independence by the Treaty of Paris in 1783. Under the treaty's terms, the new nation's western border was set at the Mississippi River. This put Michigan, as part of the Northwest Territory, under American rule.

However, British troops remained in the forts at Michilimackinac and Detroit. This was humiliating, but the new nation's government, struggling with greater problems, could do nothing about it.

Finally, in 1795, the British agreed to evacuate their outposts in the Northwest Territory as part of a treaty negotiated by Secretary of State John Jay. At noon on July 11, 1796, the British marched out of the fort at Detroit, and Captain Moses Porter of the United States Army ran the Stars and Stripes up the flagpole, more than a decade after the end of the Revolutionary War.

**From the top: The flags of Great Britain, France, Spain, and the newly founded United States as they appeared over Michigan in the late 1700s.**

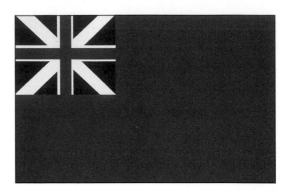

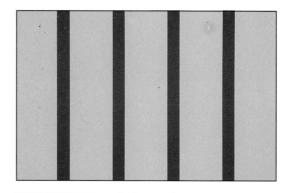

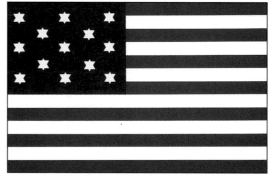

# Michigan Becomes American

The Northwest Territory, which included Michigan, was a huge triangle of western wilderness bounded by the Ohio and Mississippi rivers and the Great Lakes.

Until 1800, most of present-day Michigan was organized as Wayne County, named in honor of the general who had overseen the region's transfer to the United States. Then Congress reorganized the Northwest Territory, calling the western half, Michigan included, the Indiana Territory. Finally, in 1805, the Michigan Territory was organized.

Detroit, still the only community of any size in the sparsely settled region, became the new territory's capital. But when territorial governor William Hull arrived in Detroit in July 1805, the town was little more than charred ruins. Two weeks earlier, a fire in a stable had gone out of control and leveled the settlement.

Agustus Woodward, a territorial judge, drew up plans for the new Detroit. Inspired by the design of Washington, D.C., Woodward laid out a city of broad avenues. The judge's plan wasn't followed in full, but it provided a framework for the rebuilt city's development.

One of Detroit's leading citizens at this time was an energetic French

General Anthony Wayne (1745–96) won the nickname "Mad Anthony" after a daring night attack on a British fort in the Revolutionary War. The Native Americans he fought in the 1790s called him "the chief who never sleeps." Wayne's victories over the Native Americans secured the Northwest Territory, including Michigan, for white settlement.

Catholic priest, Gabriel Richard. Father Richard played a major role in the rebuilding of Detroit, and the words he spoke in the aftermath of the fire—"We hope for better things; it will arise from its ashes"—became part of the city's official seal.

Outside Detroit, however, Michigan was almost all wilderness. Furs remained the territory's main export, and beaver skins were used in place of money in Detroit's stores. Profits from beaver pelts led businessman John Jacob Astor to take an interest in the new territory, and in 1808 Astor's American Fur Company set up a trading post on Mackinac Island.

While Detroit began rising from the ashes, the United States and Great Britain moved toward war. Americans protested Britain's practice of kidnapping American sailors to man the ships of its own Royal Navy. They also suspected the British of arming Native Americans and encouraging them to attack settlements on America's western frontier. And many Americans saw a war with Britain as a golden opportunity to seize Canada.

**After Michigan became American territory, the federal government permitted only American fur traders in the region. This Currier & Ives lithograph shows two trappers about to skin a beaver in the Northern wilds.**

War came in the summer of 1812, and it began badly for Michigan. British troops and their Native American allies quickly captured Mackinac Island. Not long afterward, the American commander at Detroit, General William Hull, surrendered the city without firing a shot at the invading British. Once again the British flag flew over Michigan.

After a year of British occupation, the tide of war changed in favor of the United States. Whoever controlled Lake Erie controlled Michigan, and an American naval victory on the lake in September 1813 forced the British to lose their hold on the territory. On September 29, General William Henry Harrison's troops marched into Detroit, and Michigan was back under the stars and stripes.

The aftermath of the War of 1812 was a grim time for Michigan. The British occupation had been harsh, and they had looted Detroit and burned many of its buildings before leaving. For the second time in less than a decade, much of the territory's only major settlement lay in ruins.

**On September 10, 1813, an American fleet commanded by Commodore Oliver Hazard Perry clashed with British warships on Lake Erie. Perry prevailed in this three-hour battle, forcing the British to withdraw and opening the way for the American reoccupation of Detroit.**

# Settlement and Statehood

Michigan needed strong leadership if it was to recover. It got this leadership in the form of General Lewis Cass, commander of the 1,000 American troops who were stationed in Detroit following the city's rescue from the British.

Cass was appointed territorial governor and a final peace treaty was signed at the end of 1814. Governor Cass's first task was simply keeping Detroit's many hungry and homeless citizens alive until the town could again be rebuilt.

With Detroit back on its feet, Cass turned to a larger task. The Michigan Territory remained wild and unsettled, although farms and towns were spreading across other parts of the Northwest. This lack of settlement was largely because of the territory's reputation as a region unfit for farming. A government report in 1815 even called Michigan "swampy" with "sterility of soil."

In 1820, Cass decided to see for himself just what the territory had to offer settlers. With a party that included geologist Henry Rowe Schoolcraft, the governor set out on an exploring expedition. On foot and in canoes, Cass and his comrades explored the length and breadth of the territory, preparing detailed maps, cataloging its resources, and recording the beliefs

Michigan's territorial governor, Lewis Cass (1782–1866), was elected to the U.S. Senate in 1844, but later resigned to run as the Democratic candidate in the presidential election of 1848. Defeated by Zachary Taylor, he returned to the Senate the following year.

and customs of the Native Americans they encountered.

The reports of the Cass Expedition painted a much brighter picture than the earlier government accounts. Schoolcraft found rich deposits of minerals. The party found many areas of fertile soil, with plenty of water for crops. The dense forests that covered much of the state were an obstacle to farming, but Cass believed that pioneers who cleared land would be rewarded by fine harvests.

When the Cass Expedition's findings reached the East, pioneer families finally began journeying westward into the Michigan Territory. Most arrived by way of Detroit to buy public land. The first land office in the town had opened in 1818.

Much of the land now open to settlers had belonged to Michigan's remaining Native Americans. From 1819 to 1821, however, Governor Cass had persuaded many Native American leaders to sign over their lands to the territorial government.

Cass's favorite form of persuasion was rum, with which he got chiefs drunk during treaty negotiations. If rum didn't work, Cass sometimes sent troops to force Native Americans from their homelands and "escort" them to reservations farther west.

Settlement was still sparse in the early 1820s, however, because of the difficult and dangerous journey required to reach the territory. Two events changed that situation.

**This illustration of a Native American medicine man appeared in Schoolcraft's monumental book, *History, Condition and Prospects of the Indian Tribes of the United States,* which was published following the Cass Expedition.**

The first was the appearance of steamboats on the Great Lakes. The first such vessel to appear off Michigan's shores, the *Walk-In-The-Water*, docked at Detroit in 1818. Within a few years a regular steamboat route connected Detroit with other lakeside cities like Buffalo, New York.

The second event was the opening of the Erie Canal in 1825. The canal, dug across New York State to link the Great Lakes to the Atlantic, made travel to Michigan from New England and New York State much faster and easier.

This great wave of New Englanders and New Yorkers soon spread a network of tidy farms and small towns throughout the Lower Peninsula. These pioneers brought with them the traditions of their home regions—self-government, respect for education, and opposition to slavery.

In 1831, Governor Cass stepped down after eighteen years as territorial governor. His successor was George Porter. Porter, however, was often out of the territory on business. The territorial secretary, Stevens Mason, became acting governor.

Mason was only nineteen years old, so Michigan was governed by some-

**Although steamboats were not used on the Erie Canal for fear their paddles would destroy the earthen walls, they were a common sight on the Great Lakes by the mid-1800s.**

one who wasn't even legally allowed to vote! Despite his youth, Mason was an able administrator, and he quickly won the confidence of the territory's citizens.

Disaster again struck Detroit in 1832, when a boatload of sick soldiers arrived there. Soon a contagious and deadly disease—cholera—began ravaging the city and surrounding settlements. Thousands died before the epidemic ran its course. Among the victims was old Father Gabriel Richard, exhausted from long hours nursing the sick and bringing comfort to the dying.

The Michigan Territory's population tripled in the 1820s. By the mid-1830s about 30,000 people lived in the territory—many more than were needed to qualify for statehood. In 1835, the territory's voters adopted a constitution, elected Stevens Mason governor, and confidently applied for admission to the Union.

That goal, however, was delayed for two years because of two political battles. One centered on the "Toledo Strip," a section of land along Lake Erie claimed by both the Michigan Territory and the state of Ohio. Neither Ohio nor Michigan wanted to give up the strip, and at one point it looked as if Ohioans and Michiganders would actually go to war over it.

Finally, however, Michigan recognized Ohio's claim to the strip. In return, the federal government transferred a vast stretch of land—now the

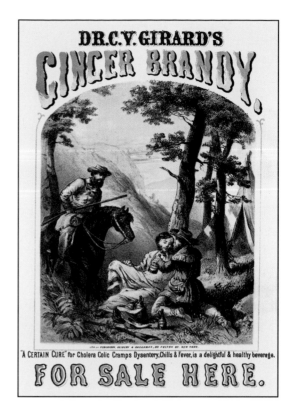

Ravaged by illness and without a known effective treatment, cholera victims often turned to homemade remedies to fight the disease.

western part of the Upper Peninsula—to Michigan.

The next hurdle on the road to statehood had to do with slavery. At this time in American history, the usual practice was to admit new states in pairs—one slave state, one free state—to keep the number of representatives in Congress balanced. Arkansas, a slave state, had to achieve statehood before Congress agreed to admit Michigan to the Union. Finally, in January 1837, Michigan became the twenty-sixth state.

# Green Gold and Mineral Mountains

The new state's first years were rocky. A nationwide economic slump set in the very year Michigan was admitted to the Union. Banks and businesses failed, and the state's supply of money and credit dried up. Michigan's government had planned a program of internal improvements, including the building of more roads and railroad tracks. These had to be put on hold until the state's financial prospects improved.

Michigan was also a cause of tension between the United States and Canada, then a British colony. In the late 1830s, some Canadians wanted to overthrow the British and achieve independence in the same way the United States had sixty years earlier. These Canadian rebels had plenty of American friends in and around the city of Detroit.

In 1838, American supporters of the rebels broke into the city's arsenal, stole weapons, and prepared to invade Canada. A small group actually crossed into Ontario later that year, but their raid was unsuccessful. Acting with great patience, Governor Mason managed to prevent many more raids and to keep the 1838 incidents from flaring into an international crisis.

In February 1841, Dr. Douglass Houghton, the state geologist, reported that he had discovered huge deposits of copper and traces of iron ore on the Upper Peninsula. Three years later, geologist William Burt found more deposits of copper and iron on the Keweenaw Peninsula and Isle Royale. These two areas had only recently been ceded to the state by the Native Americans.

Houghton's and Burt's discoveries laid the foundations for the Upper Peninsula's great mining industry. By the end of the decade, several important copper and iron mines were operating on the peninsula. Many of the original miners were immigrants from the Netherlands.

At the same time, the state's great hardwood forests began to be logged on a large scale. By 1858, more than 500 sawmills were busily turning trees, or "green gold," into lumber.

The boom in minerals and lumber helped revive the state's economy and resulted in the spread of new towns and villages across the thinly settled Upper Peninsula.

As the farms of lower Michigan continued to prosper, the state's original pioneers were joined by growing numbers of immigrants from overseas—mainly from the Netherlands, Germany, Scandinavia, and the British Isles. By 1850 Michigan's population was nearing the 400,000 mark.

**Sleighs haul logs from a Michigan forest. The Saginaw River region was the focus of the state's logging industry before the Civil War. More than 70 sawmills lined the river by 1860.**

The state had a new capital, too. In the 1840s, the state government decided to move from Detroit, but the legislature couldn't decide which town would be the new capital. Finally, the tiny settlement of Lansing—little more than a couple of houses in a forest clearing—was chosen. A state house was built, and in 1848 the legislature met for the first time at the "capital in the forest."

The 1850s was a prosperous decade for Michigan. Towns like Kalamazoo, Ann Arbor (home of the state university), and Saginaw began to thrive. Advances in transportation, like the newly built railroads, helped trade. So did the Soo Canal, which opened in 1855. The mile-long canal allowed ships on Lake Superior to bypass the rapids of the Sault Sainte Marie and descend into the other Great Lakes. From there they could reach the Atlantic Ocean by way of the Erie Canal.

Despite this progress, the 1850s saw Michigan, and the entire nation, move steadily toward a great crisis—the Civil War.

**The first railroad to reach Michigan began operating in 1836. Soon several more lines connected the state with New York and the rest of the nation, making settlement easier.**

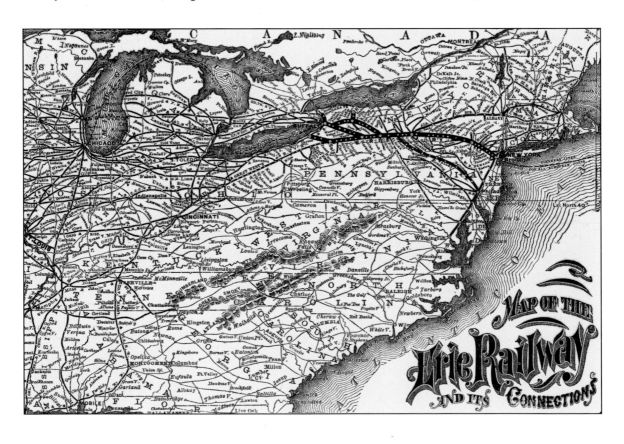

Most Michiganders were opposed to slavery, a reflection of the New England heritage of many of the state's citizens. When a new political party, the Republican Party, was formed in the mid-1850s to oppose the spread of slavery, it won immediate support in Michigan. Some people even claim that the party was founded in Jackson in 1854.

Michigan elected the nation's first Republican governor in that same year, and the party also gained a majority in the legislature.

When Republican Abraham Lincoln won the presidential election in 1860, Southern states began seceding (leaving) the Union to form the Confederate States of America. In April 1861, the conflict between the North and South flared into war.

Young Michigan men poured into Union recruiting offices. About 90,000 Michiganders fought in the conflict, out of a total 1860 population of 750,000. Combat, wounds, and disease claimed the lives of 14,000 before the Confederacy finally surrendered in April 1865.

**Michigan raised over forty regiments during the Civil War. The 21st Michigan distinguished itself during heavy fighting at Murfreesboro, Tennessee on December 31, 1862.**

# Immigration and Industry

The timber and mineral boom that began before the Civil War went into high gear after the conflict ended. In the last decades of the 19th century, millions of immigrants swelled the cities of the East, while vast western territories began to be settled. All this created a demand for the products of Michigan's mines, sawmills, work-shops, and farms.

This growth wasn't without set-backs. In 1871, for example, forest fires swept across Michigan's timber-lands, turning millions of dollars worth of lumber into ashes. In 1873, and again in 1893, national depres-sions caused financial problems for the state and hardship for many of its citizens. And in 1885, strikes by lum-ber workers seeking a ten-hour work day swept the state's sawmills and log-ging camps.

Neither forest fires, bank failures, nor strikes, however, did more than temporarily slow Michigan's growth. Production soared in the region. In the 1870s alone, Michigan led the nation in copper production; lumber mills cut more than 20 million board-feet per year; an average of 1,800 ships carried $50 million dollars worth of products out of the state's ports each year; and iron mining began on a huge scale in the Upper Peninsula's Menominee Range.

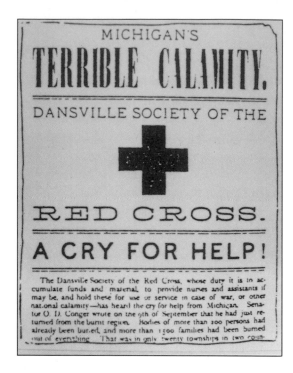

This leaflet was published by the newly found-ed American Red Cross to raise funds for vic-tims of the forest fires that blazed through Michigan in October 1871. Together, the fires claimed more than 100 lives and left about 20,000 Michiganders homeless.

Between 1870 and 1890 Michigan's population doubled, from just over 1 million in 1870 to more than 2 million in 1890. Much of this growth came from overseas immigrants who had heard of the opportunities in Michigan and were anxious to share in the economic boom. The arrival of these newcomers made the state's population more diverse. Scandinavians (especially Finns) and people from Wales and Cornwall in Britain found new homes in the mining settlements of the Upper Peninsula. Irish, Italian, and Central European immigrants arrived in the towns of Lower Michigan.

Although all the wealth brought by timber and minerals resulted in the development of some cities and towns, Michigan remained a mostly rural state in these years. Until the 1890s, about three-quarters of Michigan's population was rural. Farming remained important to the state's economy, and fruits, concentrated in lower Michigan, joined grains and vegetables as major crops.

By the turn of the 20th century much of the fresh produce of Michigan's farms stayed in the state for processing.

In 1876, Dr. John Harvey Kellogg opened a sanitarium (health resort) in Battle Creek. In the mid-1890s, Dr. Kellogg's ideas about proper nutrition inspired his brother, Will Keith Kellogg, and Charles W. Post, a former patient at the sanitarium, to found

Dr. John Harvey Kellogg (1852-1943) in academic robes. Dr. Kellogg inspired his brother Will Keith Kellogg (1860-1951) to develop cornflakes and establish one of America's best-known food-processing companies.

companies which turned oats, wheat, and corn into beverages, ready-to-eat breakfast cereals, and other nutritious foods. These products sold widely across the nation. Soon, Kellogg and C.W. Post were household names, and Battle Creek became one of the leading food-processing centers in the nation.

While Michigan's food-processing industry was on the rise, the state's logging industry suffered several setbacks and went into sharp decline.

Charles William Post (1854-1914) first gained recognition for his invention of the coffee substitute, Postum. Partly due to aggressive advertising, Postum was highly successful and was soon followed by the breakfast foods that eventually made Post a fortune.

For more than half a century, logging companies had cut down acre after acre of timber, with much more attention to profit than to replanting or other methods of conserving this valuable resource.

The result was an environmental disaster that struck in the 1890s. Much of the state's timberland was logged out, leaving only a wasteland where forests had once stood. Erosion and other damage to the soil made much of the former timberland unfit for farming. So, in the first decade of the 1900s the lumber industry moved westward to the forests of Oregon and Washington. Michigan's era of green gold was over.

At the same time, the era of Hazen W. Pingree was beginning. A Republican, Pingree was elected mayor of Detroit in 1890. Four years later he won national attention by growing potatoes in the city's vacant lots to help feed hungry victims of the Depression of 1893. He also fought corruption in the city government and pushed through many important social welfare reforms, including regulation of utilities like gas, heat, water, and electricity.

Pingree continued these reform efforts statewide after his election as governor in 1896. He became governor while still mayor of Detroit, and held both jobs until the U.S. Supreme Court decided he couldn't be both mayor and governor. Pingree kept the governorship.

# PART TWO

# 20TH CENTURY MICHIGAN

Cranbrook, a private estate in Bloomfield Hills, was one of many beautiful residences built in the Detroit suburbs around the turn of the century. It is now both an educational center and museum.

The rise of the auto industry in the first decades of the 20th century transformed Michigan from a mostly rural state to an industrial powerhouse. Although Michigan's people suffered greatly in the depression of the 1930s, the state's mighty industries made Michigan an "arsenal of democracy" for the U.S. and its allies in World War II. Prosperity continued in the postwar decades, but the social problems and racial tensions that developed in the 1960s continue today. The energy crisis of the 1970s sent the state's important auto industry into a slump that lasted into the 1980s. In recent years, however, a growing diversity of industry has revived the state's economy.

# The Coming of the Automobile

In the last decade of the 19th century and the first decade of the 20th, Michigan took the lead in a revolution that would transform the way Americans work, travel, and play—the coming of the car.

The idea of the automobile—a self-propelled vehicle that did not need rails to move from place to place—was not new. Such vehicles, most of them powered by steam, had first appeared in the late 1700s, but they were clumsy and inefficient.

In the 1870s and 80s, the development of the internal-combustion engine which creates drive power by burning fuel inside the engine provided an improved power plant. It wasn't long before inventors in Europe and America began mounting internal-combustion engines on wheels to create the first "horseless carriages."

In an amazing historical coincidence, three Michigan inventors, each working separately, produced working cars in the year 1896. The first was Charles King, who built a gas-powered car in a Detroit machine shop and drove it through the city's streets on March 1, 1896.

The second was Ransom E. Olds. Three years after constructing his first experimental automobile, Olds set up a factory in Detroit to manufacture cars. By the time he moved his factory

Henry Ford (1863-1947), the man who put America on wheels, was an often controversial figure. A man of strong and sometimes unpopular or even offensive opinions, he battled journalists, politicians, and labor leaders as well as competing auto manufacturers.

to Lansing in 1902, he had sold 3,000 Oldsmobiles and established Michigan's auto industry, soon to be the mightiest in the world.

But, it was the third inventor, Henry Ford, who had the greatest impact. Born in 1863 and raised on a farm near Dearborn, Ford was fascinated by machinery and spent his boyhood tinkering and experimenting. Moving to Detroit at the age of fourteen, he honed his mechanical skills in the city's busy machine shops.

By the 1890s Ford was an accomplished engineer with a job running the city's electrical generating plants.

The idea of the automobile obsessed Ford. With the help of his wife, Clara, he spent almost three years creating a four-wheel, gas-powered car—the Quadricycle—in a shed behind the couple's house. On the morning of June 4, 1896, Ford drove his Quadricycle onto the street.

Not until 1899, however, did Ford go full-time into car making. He set up two companies to manufacture Ford-designed cars. Both failed because of business problems. In 1903, Ford and several investors established the Ford Motor Company.

This venture was a success, but Ford wasn't satisfied. By now, automobiles were a common sight. But they were far too expensive for the average American, and most people considered them "rich people's toys" with little practical value. Ford decided to change that. He set about designing a simple, sturdy car that could be mass-produced and inexpensive. The result was the now famous Model T.

**The 1896 Quadricycle, Ford's first car. According to some accounts, Ford built the car in a shed behind his house without first measuring the door. He then had to batter down a wall to move his landmark vehicle to the street.**

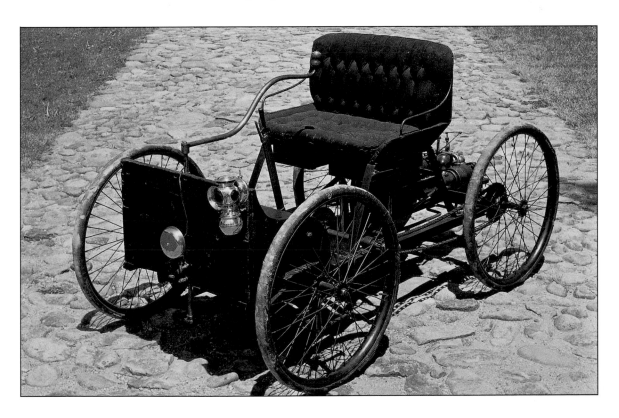

The first T rolled off the production line at Ford's Highland Park plant in October 1908. The car was a no-frills vehicle (buyers had to pay extra for a windshield and headlights), but at $850 for the four-seat model, the Model T was a great success.

The Model T took America by storm. By 1913, demand was so high that Ford redesigned the Highland Park assembly line using innovative mass-production methods. Within a year the plant was building cars at the rate of one every 98 minutes. In 1915, the millionth Model T left the plant. The more Ts Ford sold, the lower he could price the car; the 1915 version cost $440, and in the 1920s the price dropped to $220.

Meanwhile, other carmakers were busily turning Detroit into America's Motor City. In 1908, William C. Durant merged several car makers (including Olds) to form General Motors. In the 1920s, Walter Chrysler established the company that still bears his name. This completed the Big Three—Ford, General Motors, and Chrysler—that still dominates America's auto industry today.

Michigan was an ideal state for car manufacturing because it had plenty

**Ford produced several versions of the Model T, including the delivery van shown in this advertisement (top left), but they were all no-frills.**

**The motorized assembly line at Ford's Highland Park plant (bottom left). In this 1913 photograph, workers fit wheels to Model T bodies.**

of iron ore, the chief ingredient for steel, within its borders. Also, Michigan was close to other iron-producing states, like Minnesota. The Great Lakes were an easy means of bringing raw materials into the state.

The auto boom transformed Michigan society. Thousands of Michiganders moved from rural areas to take jobs in the car and auto-part plants of Detroit, Lansing, Pontiac, Flint, and other cities.

Many more poured in from across the country, including thousands of African Americans from the Southern states. Detroit's African-American population increased eightfold between 1910 and 1920.

America's entry into World War I gave a boost not only to Michigan's manufacturing but to its agriculture and food-processing industries, too. But it was the automobile boom that powered the state's economy. By 1920, carmaking was a $1-billion industry employing more than 150,000 people.

Those numbers rose dramatically during the 1920s, a generally prosperous decade when, for the first time, many working Americans found they could afford a car.

**Henry Ford initially opposed World War I. When America entered the conflict in 1917, however, Ford began production of military hardware, including the tank shown here.**

# Michigan in Depression and War

Between 1900 and 1929, Michigan's population doubled to about 4.8 million, thanks both to migration of people from other states and immigration from overseas. Newcomers from Italy and from Central and Eastern Europe—especially Poland—poured in to take advantage of the jobs in Michigan's factories.

The population boom was especially great in the cities of Michigan. At the turn of the century three-quarters of Michigan's people lived in rural areas; by 1930 less than a third did, and Detroit's population alone reached 1.5 million.

In 1900, Michigan's wealth came mostly from farming and the tapping of natural resources like iron ore and copper. By 1929, manufacturing claimed the greatest share of the state's economy. In addition to car manufacturing, Michigan's factories, mills, and machine shops turned out everything from refrigerators to airplanes.

The year 1929, however, saw the beginning of a crisis that would bring the industrial giant of Michigan to its knees and reduce many of its citizens to poverty and despair.

On October 24 of that year, a day known as "Black Thursday," the New York Stock Exchange crashed and the prosperity of the 1920s reached its end. Over the next couple of years a deep economic depression spread over the country.

No state suffered more than Michigan during the Great Depression. With millions of people out of work, car sales dropped, and so did orders for other goods. By 1932, factories had shut down and more than 40 percent of workers in Michigan's major cities were unemployed. Total unemployment across the state hit 20 percent in 1935.

Many Michiganders left their home state in a desperate search for work in other parts of the country. Michigan's population fell by almost 30 percent in the early 1930s.

State programs and the federal New Deal agencies set up by President Franklin D. Roosevelt provided some relief to the hungry, but the economic picture remained bleak. In Detroit, thousands of jobless workers lined up at soup kitchens and slept in ware-

**Reginald Marsh drew this haunting portrayal of unemployed people lining up at a soup kitchen during the Great Depression (top right). In 1933 Michigan's State Emergency Welfare Commission, an agency set up to deal with the crisis, found that 640,000 Michiganders depended on the government to prevent starvation.**

**As the Depression worsened the unemployed grew desperate. On March 7, 1932, 3,000 jobless men went on a "hunger march" to the Ford Motor Company's River Rouge plant (bottom right). Demanding work, they wished to present a petition at the plant but were turned back by Dearborn police.**

houses that had been full of gleaming new cars just a few years before.

Even those workers lucky enough to keep their homes and jobs had to endure reduced hours and wages. In the automobile factories, unsafe conditions prevailed and production lines were sped up as managers tried to cut costs by making more cars with fewer workers. Protesting these conditions, workers often turned Michigan's car plants into bloody battlegrounds in the 1930s: Workers and labor-union organizers were on one side; company owners and managers on the other.

The Big Three carmakers refused to recognize the United Auto Workers union as representing their workers' interests. But the UAW had a determined leader—Walter Reuther, a former toolmaker. In 1936, the UAW joined the powerful Congress of Industrial Organizations (CIO), a collection of unions.

In December of that year, the UAW went on strike at the General Motors plant in Flint. Here, Reuther introduced a new tactic—the sit-down strike. Instead of not showing up for work, the strikers simply occupied the factory. Reuther's theory was this: "If the boss won't talk, don't take a walk—sit down!"

Angry GM executives urged newly elected governor Frank Murphy to order the National Guard to drive the strikers out of the occupied buildings. Murphy refused and instead brought both sides to the bargaining table.

**One of the most important leaders in the history of organized labor, Walter Reuther (1907–70) served as president of the United Auto Workers (UAW) for almost twenty-five years. Reuther was also president of the Congress of Industrial Organizations (CIO), the successor to the Committee of Industrial Organizations, for four years.**

The strike ended in February 1937 with General Motors finally agreeing to recognize the UAW. A similar strike against Chrysler in Detroit led the second of the Big Three automakers to recognize the United Auto Workers.

But Ford held out against the union. Union men were brutally treated when they tried to organize—Reuther himself was beaten up by Ford "security guards" in May 1937. It wasn't until 1941 that the last of the Big Three accepted the UAW, and only then because of action by the state government and the U.S. Supreme Court.

Thanks to the UAW, working conditions and wages slowly improved for Michigan's auto workers. Statewide, however, Michigan's economy didn't recover until World War II. The recovery began when the nation began the process of rearmament to prepare against the threat from overseas. After the U.S. finally entered the war itself in December 1941, production increased dramatically.

Almost overnight, auto plants converted to defense production—tanks, trucks, aircraft, landing craft, and naval vessels—not just for the U.S. military, but for American allies like the Soviet Union and Great Britain. Altogether, Michigan industry accounted for 12 percent of all the war materials produced in the entire United States—by far the greatest industrial contribution of any state.

This World War II poster heralds the Civil Air Patrol, which maintained home security and guarded the civilian skies. Aircraft and other military equipment were necessary both for the fight abroad and for the protection of the people at home.

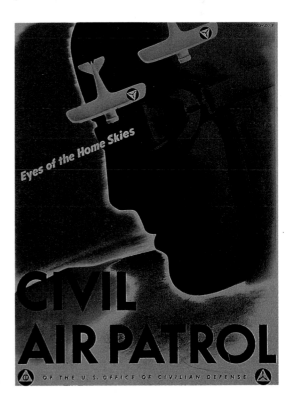

Factories that had been shut down for much of the 1930s now ran full blast 24 hours a day. Once again, people from all over the country came to Michigan's cities to work. Among them were thousands of African Americans who hoped to share in the wartime boom.

Most were bitterly disappointed. Only a third of Detroit-area defense plants would hire African Americans at all, and even in those they generally got only the worst-paid and lowest-skilled jobs. And although Michigan had no legal system of segregation (separation of races), African Americans were restricted to their own neighborhoods and often faced angry whites when they ventured out of them.

Wartime racial tensions in Detroit came to a head on a hot July night in 1943 when a fight between a white man and an African American in Belle Isle Park sparked the worst race riot the country had seen up until then. Violence swept the streets of Detroit for two nights. Before troops moved in to restore peace, thirty-four people (most of them African Americans) had been killed. Hundreds more were injured.

The 1943 riot was a blot on Michigan's otherwise spectacular contribution to the war effort. Besides the state's massive output of defense goods, some 600,000 Michiganders of all races served in the military. About 15,000 lost their lives.

The front page of the *Detroit News* reports the June 1943 riot. After the riot, Mayor Edward Jeffries and UAW official R. J. Thomas formed a committee of Detroit citizens in an effort to ease racial tensions and prevent further outbreaks of violence.

# The Prosperous Postwar Years

Peace came in August 1945. Although this resulted in a decrease in defense production, prosperity did not diminish for Michigan. After military personnel returned home, there was an increased demand for automobiles and other civilian products. Michigan's auto plants were quickly converted to meet the demand.

America was now a car culture, and the period from the mid-1940s to the mid-1960s was perhaps the golden age of American cars. With oil and gas prices low, cars grew bigger, faster, fancier, and flashier. Auto designers and engineers like General Motors's flamboyant Harley Earl added ever more outlandish features—tail fins, wraparound windshields, eye-catching paint jobs, dashboards loaded with gadgets and gizmos—to every new model.

Americans bought these sleek, supercharged cars in record numbers. In 1955 alone, Michigan's auto plants produced more than 9 million cars.

A sign of the importance of Michigan's auto industry to the country came in 1953 when GM president Charles E. Wilson became secretary of defense in President Dwight Eisenhower's cabinet. "What's good for General Motors is what's good for the country," Wilson reportedly said when he accepted the post.

A scientist at the Chrysler Corporation's research laboratory works on a formula for rust-resistant paint in this 1954 photograph. Michigan's auto manufacturers depended on the work of people in a variety of related industries and activities, like the research shown here.

The bitter labor struggles of the 1930s were a thing of the past, too. The workingman was no longer helpless in the face of the corporation. By the 1950s, the United Auto Workers numbered more than 1.6 million members in Michigan and other states. With this powerful support, Walter Reuther was in a position to negotiate a series of landmark agreements with the Big Three.

Starting in 1948, UAW contracts regularly included items like profit-sharing for employees, guaranteed yearly raises, and generous benefits in the event of layoffs. These contracts (some of which remained in effect until the 1980s) were an enormous victory for the UAW, and made Detroit's auto workers the envy of many working Americans.

With improved working conditions and high rates of production, Michigan's towns and cities continued to grow in the decades following World War II. The Lower Peninsula experienced widespread suburbanization, as people moved to neighborhoods outside the city limits and rings of residential communities sprang up around Detroit, Grand Rapids, Lansing, and other cities.

An unfortunate aspect of this trend, especially for Detroit, was that it tended to leave inner-city areas with fewer tax dollars, and the people remaining in these areas were often poor and African American. This helped create the conditions that would eventually lead to racial unrest and urban decay.

Trouble also appeared in the form of natural disasters which struck Michigan twice in the 1950s. In June 1953 and again in April 1956, powerful tornadoes roared across the state. More than a hundred people in Flint were killed in the 1953 episode, and eighteen people in Grand Rapids lost their lives in the second.

Michigan gave the nation a number of important political figures in the post–World War II years.

In 1949, a young former University of Michigan football player named Gerald Ford began the first of twenty-four years' service in the House of Representatives. Appointed vice president in 1973, he became the president in 1974 following Nixon's resignation and was the first Michigan resident in the White House.

In the same year that Gerald Ford entered the House of Representatives, the North Atlantic Treaty Organization (NATO), an important defense association of North American and European countries, came into being. Arthur Vandenburg, a Michigan senator at the time, was one of NATO's chief architects.

Detroit-born Ralph Bunche became the first African American to

**Gerald Ford as a young congressman poses outside the Capitol building in Washington, D.C. He holds a license plate promoting his home state's fruit industry.**

hold important diplomatic posts. In 1950, Bunche won the Nobel Peace Prize for his work as a United Nations mediator in the conflict between Arabs and Jews in the newly-founded state of Israel. Seventeen years later, he was appointed undersecretary to the United Nations.

Michigan's governor from 1949 to 1961 was G. Mennen Williams. In 1957 Governor Williams was on hand to open a structure one newspaper called "a wedding ring for the state"—the majestic Mackinac Bridge. "Mighty Mac" took three years to build and spanned the Straits of Mackinac, linking the Upper and Lower Peninsulas for the first time in history.

In the early 1960s, pop music joined cars as a major product of Detroit. Berry Gordy, Jr., a former Ford assembly-line worker, began recording local African-American musicians and singing groups in 1959. His Motown Records (from "Motor Town," another nickname for Detroit) rose to the top with its number-one hits scored by the Supremes, a trio led by Diana Ross.

Throughout the 1960s and 1970s, Motown brought the soulful, energetic music of artists like Stevie Wonder, Marvin Gaye, and The Jackson Five to the world. In the process, Berry Gordy's Motown Records became one of America's most successful African-American companies.

The Supremes, Motown's star performers in the 1960s, released no fewer than twelve number-one hits during that decade. Lead singer Diana Ross went on to solo success as a singer and actress after the group's breakup.

# Times of Trouble, Times of Change

In the early 1960s, Michigan's state government carried out some significant reforms. Faced with a shortage of money, the government adopted an income tax for the first time in 1963. In the same year, Michigan's citizens voted to draft a new state constitution. Michigan was governed by a constitution adopted in 1908, and many Michiganders felt it didn't meet the needs of a modern, urban industrialized state.

The new state constitution became law in 1964 during the governorship of George W. Romney, a former auto executive. A Republican, Romney was a contender for his party's presidential nomination in the election of 1968, but he ultimately lost the nomination to Richard Nixon.

The state's auto-powered economy continued to thrive in the early 1960s, but by the middle of the decade the first signs of trouble began to appear.

In 1965, a lawyer named Ralph Nader published *Unsafe at Any Speed*, a book in which he claimed that Detroit knowingly marketed unsafe, poorly designed cars, causing much unnecessary death and injury. Nader singled out for criticism the Ford Mustang, brainchild of a Ford executive named Lee Iacocca, and General Motors's Corvair.

Ralph Nader's *Unsafe at Any Speed* raised important concerns about Detroit's auto industry and launched Nader on a career as a consumer advocate and reformer. Here, Nader is testifying before a congressional committee.

Although *Unsafe at Any Speed* did not have much impact on Mustang sales, sales of GM's Corvair dropped 93 percent, demonstrating that many Americans had begun to wonder if what was good for Detroit's car makers was really good for the country.

In the mid-1960s, however, most Michiganders were more concerned with racial tensions in their cities than with the impact of car safety problems on the auto industry.

By 1960, Detroit, once America's third-largest city, had fallen to fourth place. While Detroit's suburbs continued to grow, its mostly poor, mostly African-American inner-city neighborhoods slipped further into decline. Crime and unemployment rates were high; opportunities for education and advancement were few. Many of the people in these areas felt they were cut off from the mainstream of Michigan society and denied a share in the prosperity much of the state enjoyed.

As in 1943, tensions finally turned into violence. In July 1967 riots broke out in Detroit. In disturbances that lasted a full week, shops were looted, buildings were burned, and

A striking interior view of the Renaissance Center, showing the complex's prestressed concrete columns and dramatic exposed walkways (top right). The RenCen includes five office towers, a hotel, and parking space for 6,000 cars.

Coleman Young, Detroit's first African-American mayor, served in office for two decades (bottom right).

gunfights raged between rioters and policemen.

By the time the riots ended, whole blocks of the city lay in ruins. Some $50 million in property was destroyed. Forty-three were dead. As in 1943, most of those killed were African Americans. In human terms, the 1967 riot was the worst in American history until the Los Angeles riots of 1992.

Six years later, in 1973, Detroit (by then more than 60 percent African American) elected its first African-American mayor, Coleman Young. With the help of business leaders like Henry Ford II, grandson of the company founder, the new mayor worked to revive Detroit. The mid-1970s saw an ambitious program of urban renewal, capped in 1977 by the opening of the $350 million Renaissance Center office-hotel complex on the Detroit River. But the Renaissance Center and similar projects could not solve continuing problems of crime and poverty.

These problems were made worse by a crisis that hit Michigan's auto industry in the early 1970s. Americans had long been used to paying low prices for oil and gasoline, and the nation had become dependent on inexpensive fuel imported from overseas. Starting in 1973, however, the Organization of Petroleum-Exporting Countries, or OPEC, began to flex its political muscles by greatly raising oil prices.

With gasoline suddenly expensive and often in short supply, Americans began to turn away from big American cars—now nicknamed "gas guzzlers"—and toward more fuel-efficient imported cars. In the 1950s, less than 5 percent of all the cars sold in the U.S. were imported. By the end of the 1970s, imports—mostly Japanese—accounted for more than 25 percent of American auto sales.

Besides the energy crisis, Michigan's auto industry had to face growing concerns over the amount of pollution given off by its products. As more and more Americans became concerned with the impact of cars on the environment, laws were passed requiring pollution-control devices in new cars. Auto-industry executives, however, often argued that these changes drove up the price of American cars, widening the market for imports.

By 1975, Michigan's auto industry was in a serious slump. Sales picked up briefly the following year, but by 1978 they were down again and would stay that way for years.

With one-third of all Michigan workers employed in auto manufacturing and related industries, the result was an economic crisis that affected the entire state. This was reflected in Michigan's rate of growth. Its population grew by just over 4 percent in the 1970s, only one-third of the average growth rate for the rest of the country.

# Michigan Today

In the early 1980s, Michigan's situation was desperate. By 1983, the state's overall unemployment rate hit 17 percent—close to the 20 percent rate reached fifty years earlier in the depths of the Great Depression. Jobless rates in the industrial cities were often even higher.

Population growth not only slowed, but the state actually lost population in the first half of the 1980s—one of only five states to do so. Michigan's economic crisis led the state government to make heavy cuts in funding for education and social programs.

At his inauguration in 1983, Governor James Blanchard told Michiganders the state needed to change, or else "we are going to be a state which time passes by."

Michiganders listened, and slowly the state—with the auto industry in the lead—adapted to changing times. The recovery process, however, was often painful.

One Michigan success story in the 1980s was the revival of the Chrysler Corporation. Lee Iacocca took over the leadership of Chrysler in the late 1970s, when the company teetered on the edge of bankruptcy. Iacocca persuaded Congress to lend Chrysler more than $1 billion to keep the company afloat while it reorganized. Under his direction, Chrysler re-

bounded, and the company was able to pay off the loan ahead of schedule. Chrysler's amazing recovery made Iacocca a hero to many Americans.

In the mid-1980s economic conditions began to improve in Michigan. The Big Three were turning out more fuel-efficient and environmentally friendly models that were better able to compete with foreign imports. A thriving national economy brought more Americans into car dealerships, sending new-car sales up once more. As a result, in the late 1980s car production increased. Production fell during the recession of 1991-93, but got back on track in the mid-1990s and now is forging ahead.

Today, however, Michigan produces only about one-third of all American cars. Beginning in the late 1960s, car and car-part manufacturers moved many of their operations from Michigan to other states, especially in the South and Southwest. Car sales still have a great impact on Michigan's economy, but the effect is much less than it was in the 1970s.

Other industries have taken up the slack left by the departure of much of the auto industry. Furniture making and food processing, industries established in the 19th century, contribute greatly to Michigan's economy. Agriculture now accounts for only about 2 percent of the state's wealth, but Michigan's farms still produce many specialized crops, including beans and cherries.

Lee Iacocca (right) took the helm of the troubled Chrysler Corporation in 1978 and brought the company back from the brink of bankruptcy.

Today, auto manufacturers increasingly use computer-controlled robots—like those shown below, at work in a Ford plant—to build and assemble cars.

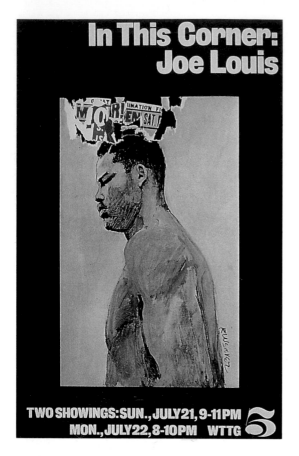

**In This Corner: Joe Louis**

TWO SHOWINGS: SUN., JULY 21, 9-11PM
MON., JULY 22, 8-10PM    WTTG 5

The construction of the Joe Louis arena sparked a revival of interest in Louis himself. Considered by some the greatest heavyweight fighter of this century, Louis was for decades a source of pride for Michiganders of all races.

In recent years the Upper Peninsula has enjoyed an energy boom, thanks to the discovery of oil and natural-gas deposits in the region. Mining has revived, too, as new, improved methods have been introduced to process low-grade ores without damaging the environment.

Environmental quality is a growing concern of Michiganders. In the 1970s, a dangerous chemical, PBB, poisoned many Michigan farm animals, and the contamination spread into the soil. The PBB problem and concerns over pollution of the state's waterways led to the introduction of many measures aimed at restoring and improving Michigan's environment.

Conservation efforts, for example, have resulted in the replanting of much of Michigan's logged-out timberland, especially on the Upper Peninsula. The restoration of this area's wild beauty has made it a favorite vacation destination, and tourism, camping, and leisure activities are now fast-growing sectors of the state's economy.

Michigan's cities, especially Detroit, continue to experience the problems common to many other major northern cities—poverty, racial tension, and high crime.

In Detroit, Coleman Young remained in the mayor's office through 1993, when he was succeeded by Dennis Archer. A program of urban renewal continued in those years, including the construction of the People Mover transit system, the Detroit Science Center, and the Joe Louis Arena, a sports facility named for the great heavyweight boxer Joe Louis (1914–81), who once lived in Detroit.

These projects helped attract some new businesses to Detroit, but the city continued to lose population. By 1990, Detroit had dropped to seventh

place among U.S. cities. A serious crime problem has contributed to Detroit's difficulties: In the 1980s and 1990s, Detroit had one of the highest rates for murder and other serious crimes in the nation.

Still, Detroit's government, business, educational, and community leaders continue to work hard at solving the city's problems. Wayne State University, in particular, is active in community programs aimed at improving conditions and providing educational opportunities for inner-city residents.

In 1990, Michiganders elected John Engler governor. A conservative Republican, Engler took office with a

**The Grand Hotel on Mackinac Island, now restored to its original splendor, attracts tourists from around the country. No cars are permitted on the island; visitors travel by horse or bicycle.**

program of wide-ranging reforms of the state's social services. Other state governments are now eagerly watching to see if Michigan's reform experiments succeed.

From the forested hills of the Upper Peninsula to the skyscrapers of downtown Detroit, Michiganders take great pride in their state. The stresses of a changing society have taken their toll, but as a new century approaches Michigan moves forward with hope and confidence.

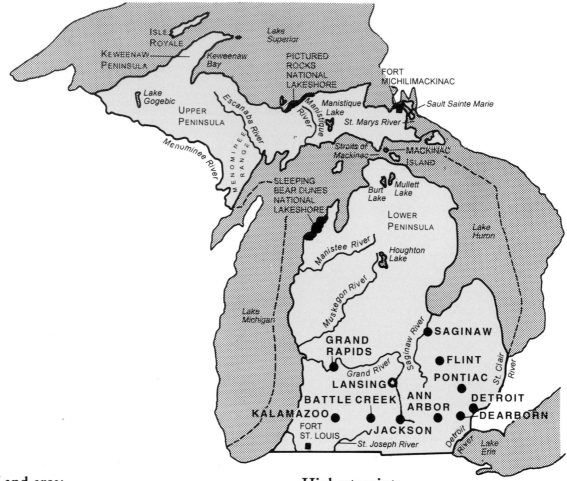

**Land area:**
56,809 square miles, plus 40,148 miles of water surface. Ranks 23rd in size.

**Major rivers:**
The Detroit; the Escanaba; the Grand; the Kalamazoo; the Manistee; the Manistique; the Menominee; the Muskegon; the Ontonagon; the Saginaw River system; the St. Clair; the St. Joseph; the St. Marys; the Sturgeon; the Tahquamenon; the Whitefish.

**Highest point:**
Mount Arvon, 1,980 ft.

**Major bodies of water:**
Burt Lake; Houghton Lake; Lake Erie; Lake Gogebic; Lake Huron; Lake Michigan; Lake Superior; Manistique Lake; Mullett Lake; Straits of Mackinac.

**Climate:**
Average January temperature: 32° F
Average July temperature: 72.3° F

**Population: 9,477,545 (1993)**
**Rank: 8th**
   1840: 212,267
   1900: 2,420,982
   1960: 7,823,194

**Population of major cities (1990):**

| | |
|---|---|
| Detroit | 1,027,974 |
| Grand Rapids | 189,126 |
| Warren | 144,864 |
| Flint | 140,761 |
| Lansing | 127,321 |
| Sterling Heights | 117,810 |
| Ann Arbor | 109,592 |

**Ethnic breakdown by percentage (1993):**

| | |
|---|---|
| White | 83.6% |
| African American | 14.5% |
| Native American | 0.6% |
| Other | 1.3% |

**Economy:**
   Manufacturing (especially cars, trucks, and other motor vehicles); Nonelectrical machinery and metalworking; Food processing (especially breakfast cereals); Industrial chemicals and compounds; Agriculture (dairy cattle, corn, vegetables); Minerals (iron ore, oil, and natural gas).

**State Government:**
   Legislature: Michigan has a bicameral (two house) legislature with a House of Representatives and a Senate. There are 38 senators elected for a four-year term, and 110 representatives, elected for a two-year term.
   Governor: Elected for a four-year term, the governor is the head of the executive branch of the state government.
   Courts: The judicial branch of Michigan's government includes district courts, circuit courts, a court of appeals, and a supreme court. The seven justices of the state supreme court are elected for eight-year terms.

**State Capital:**
   Lansing

## State Flag

Michigan's flag features a shield with the word *Tuebor* ("I will defend" in Latin) centered on a dark blue background. The shield is topped by an eagle and the motto *E Pluribus Unum* ("Out of many, one") which symbolizes the relationship between the state and national government.

## State Seal

Michigan's state seal includes a shield enclosed in a circle with the words "The Great Seal of the State of Michigan" along the top and the date 1835 in roman numerals along the bottom.

## State Motto

*Si Quaeris Peninsulam Amoenam, Circumspice.* Latin meaning: "If You Seek A Pleasant Peninsula, Look Around You."

## State Nickname

The "Wolverine State" from the wolverine pelts fur traders once traded with the region's Native Americans. Michigan is also called the "Great Lake State."

# Places

**Bay City State Park,** Bay City

**Colonial Michilimackinac,** Mackinaw City

**Cornish Pump and Mining Museum,** Iron Mountain

**Cranbrook Academy of Art,** Bloomfield Hills

**Custor Collection, Monroe County Library Stystem,** Monroe

**Detroit Institute of Arts,** Detroit

**Dodge No. 4 State Park,** Pontiac

**Dossin Great Lakes Museum,** Detroit

**Fairlane, the Henry Ford Estate,** Dearborn

**Father Marquette National Memorial and Museum,** St. Ignace

**Fort Gratiot Light,** Port Huron

**Fort Wilkins State Park,** Copper Harbor

**Gerald Ford Museum,** Grand Rapids

**Grand Haven State Park,** Grand Haven

**Henry Ford Museum and Greenfield Village,** Dearborn

**Harrisville State Park,** Harrisville

**Holly State Park,** Holly

**Interlochen Center for the Arts,** Interlochen

**Island Lake State Park,** Brighton

**Kimball House,** Battle Creek

**Kingman Museum of Natural History,** Battle Creek

## to See

Ludington State Park, Ludington

Michigan Historical Commission Archives, Lansing

Museum of Afro-American History, Detroit

Muskegon State Park, North Muskegon

Netherlands Museum and Dutch Village, Holland

Fort Mackinac, Mackinac Island

Onaway State Park, Onaway

Ortonville State Park, Ortonville

Palms Book State Park, Manistique

Pictured Rocks National Lakeshore, Munising

Pinckney State Park, Pinckney

Pontiac Lake State Park, Pontiac

Porcupine Mountains Wilderness State Park, Ontonagon

Renaissance Center, Detroit

Sleeping Bear Dunes National Lakeshore, Frankfort

Sterling State Park, Monroe

Tahquamenon Falls State Park, Paradise

Tawas Point State Park and Light, East Tawas

Warren Dunes State Park, Sawyer

Waterloo State Park, Chelsea

White Pine Village, Ludington

Yankee Air Force Museum, Ypsilanti

## State Flower

Michigan's state flower is not a garden or wildflower but the blossom of the apple tree (*Malus domestica*). The five-petaled apple blossom, which typically appears in late spring, has a beautiful white coloring streaked with pink.

## State Bird

The robin is Michigan's state bird. This common songbird is about ten inches long with a reddish breast and darker plumage along the rest of its body.

## State Tree

The Eastern white pine (*Pinus strobus*) is a tree with dark gray bark. It commonly grows to a height of between 50 and 75 feet, but some have been known to reach more than 170 feet.

# Michigan History

**1618-22** Etienne Brulé of France passes through Michigan during his exploration of the Great Lakes region

**1668** French missionary Jacques Marquette establishes the first European outpost in Michigan

**1701** Detroit is founded by Antoine de la Mothe Cadillac

**1760** The British take control of Detroit

**1763** Pontiac's "Rebellion": The British garrison at Detroit is besieged by the Ottawa leader Pontiac and his allies

**1781** Spanish forces invade Michigan during the Revolutionary War

**1783** The treaty ending the Revolutionary War makes the Great Lakes region, including present-day Michigan, U.S. territory

**1787** Congress adopts the Northwest Ordinance, organizing the Great Lakes region and establishing a form of government there

**1805** The Michigan Territory is created

**1812** Governor William Hull surrenders Detroit to the British, one of several U.S. defeats in the region in the first years of the War of 1812

**1813** American troops reenter Detroit; Lewis Cass becomes governor of Michigan Territory

# American

**1492** Christopher Columbus discovers America

**1607** Jamestown (Virginia) founded by English colonists

**1620** *Mayflower* arrives at Plymouth (Massachusetts)

**1754-63** French and Indian War

**1765** Parliament passes Stamp Act

**1775-83** Revolutionary War

**1776** Signing of the Declaration of Independence

**1788-90** First congressional elections

**1791** Bill of Rights added to U.S. Constitution

**1803** Louisiana Purchase

**1812-14** War of 1812

**1820** Missouri Compromise

**1836** Battle of the Alamo (Texas)

**1846-48** Mexican-American War

**1849** California Gold Rush

**1860** South Carolina secedes from Union

**1861-65** Civil War

**1862** Lincoln signs Homestead Act

**1863** Emancipation Proclamation

**1865** President Lincoln assassinated (April 14)

**1865-77** Reconstruction in the South

**1866** Civil Rights bill passed

**1881** President James Garfield shot (July 2)

# History

**1896** First Ford automobile is made

**1898-99** Spanish-American War

**1901** President William McKinley is shot (Sept. 6)

**1917** U.S. enters World War I

**1922** Nineteenth Amendment passed, giving women the vote

**1929** U.S. stock market crash; Great Depression begins

**1933** Franklin D. Roosevelt becomes president; begins New Deal

**1941** Japanese attack Pearl Harbor (Dec. 7); U.S. enters World War II

**1945** U.S. drops atomic bomb on Hiroshima and Nagasaki; Japan surrenders, ending World War II

**1963** President Kennedy assassinated (November 22)

**1964** Civil Rights Act passed

**1965-73** Vietnam War

**1968** Martin Luther King, Jr., shot in Memphis (April 4)

**1974** President Richard Nixon resigns because of Watergate scandal

**1979-81** Hostage crisis in Iran: 52 Americans held captive for 444 days

**1989** End of U.S.-Soviet cold war

**1991** U.S. enters Gulf War

**1995** Terrorists bomb a federal building in Oklahoma City

# Michigan History

**1835-36** Border War between Michigan and Ohio; Michigan gives up land along Lake Erie but gains most of Upper Peninsula

**1837** January 26: Michigan is admitted to the Union

**1840** Copper deposits are found on the Upper Peninsula; iron is discovered four years later

**1848** State capitol moves from Detroit to Lansing

**1871** Massive forest fires sweep across parts of the state

**1896** Henry Ford of Detroit builds his first successful car

**1908** The Model T goes into production and automobile industry goes into high gear

**1935** United Auto Workers Union (UAW), one of the nation's most powerful labor organizations, is formed

**1957** The Mackinac Bridge connects the Upper and Lower peninsulas

**1970s** Rising fuel prices and competition from imports send Michigan's auto industry into decline

**1973** Coleman Young becomes the first African-American mayor of Detroit

**1974** Gerald R. Ford becomes first Michigan resident to attain the presidency

**1985** Michigan begins to recover from economic slump of 1970s; pays off debts

**Antoine de la Mothe Cadillac (1656–1730)**
This French explorer, soldier, and colonial official established the settlement that became Detroit.

**Henry Rowe Schoolcraft (1793–1864)** Schoolcraft accompanied territorial governor Lewis Cass on his exploration of Michigan and made a valuable record of the expedition's findings.

**George Armstrong Custer (1839–76)** After graduating last in his class from West Point, this Michigan cavalryman made a name for himself as a dashing young general in the Civil War. Sent West to fight Native Americans after the Civil War ended, he was killed at the Battle of Little Bighorn in June 1876.

*George Armstrong Custer*

**Hazen S. Pingree (1840–1901)** Mayor of Detroit (1890–97) and governor of Michigan (1897–1901), Pingree was the greatest political figure of the Progressive era in Michigan. He was responsible for much reform-minded legislation.

**William C. Durant (1861–1947)** "Billy" Durant was, along with Henry Ford, one of the first industrialists to apply mass-production technology to car manufacturing. He also oversaw the merger of several carmakers into the General Motors Corporation.

**Henry Ford (1863–1947)** Born on a Dearborn farm, Ford worked as an engineer and mechanic in Detroit before building his first successful automobile in 1896. Eight years later he introduced the low-priced, easy-to-build Model T and became one of the most powerful industrialists in the world.

**John Francis Dodge (1864–1920) and Horace Elgin Dodge (1868–1920)** The Dodge brothers started in business as part suppliers to several Detroit auto manufacturers, but in 1914 they formed their own successful car company. After their deaths, Dodge was absorbed by the Chrysler Corporation.

**Ransom Eli Olds (1864–1950)** Olds built his first car (powered by steam) in Detroit in 1887, but soon turned to gas powered models. In 1904 he introduced the Oldsmobile, a low-priced car that anticipated the Model T.

**Will Keith Kellogg (1860–1951)** Kellogg helped introduce the world to prepared cereals by developing cornflakes and other products in his hometown of Battle Creek. Kellogg put his nutritional ideas into practice by working in the Battle Creek Sanitarium, a health resort run by his brother, Dr. John Harvey Kellogg (1852–1943).

**Arthur Vandenberg (1884–1951)** This Grand Rapids-born politician won a Senate seat in 1928 which he held until his death. Although known as an Isolationist (someone who opposed U.S. entry into World War II), he changed his mind after Pearl Harbor and became an important foreign-policy adviser to President Harry S. Truman.

**Bruce Catton (1899–1978)**
A native of Petoskey, Catton was perhaps the greatest historian of the Civil War. He is best known for his three-volume history of the Union's Army of the Potomac; the trilogy's final volume, *A Stillness at Appomattox* (1953), received both the Pulitzer Prize for History and the National Book Award.

**Ralph Bunche (1904–71)**
Born in Detroit, Bunche was the first African American to hold high diplomatic rank. Joining the United Nations in 1947 after teaching at both Harvard and Howard universities, Bunche won the 1950 Nobel Peace Prize for negotiating an end to the first Arab-Israeli war.

*Ralph Bunche*

**Walter Reuther (1907–70)**
Born in West Virginia, Reuther moved to Detroit as a young man and worked in auto plants while putting himself through college. Reuther led the fight to unionize the Detroit auto manufacturers in the 1930s and later served as president of the UAW and AFL-CIO.

**Alfred Day Hershey (born 1908)** A native of Owosso, Hershey is one of the most influential genetic scientists of the 20th century. A longtime director of research at several important laboratories, Hershey won a Nobel Prize in 1969 for his work on viruses.

**Joe Louis (1914–81)** Raised in Detroit, this great boxer was the longest-reigning heavyweight champion in history—he defended his title for 11 years in 25 fights. An African American, Louis became a hero to all Americans when he left the ring at the peak of his career to serve in World War II.

**Coleman Alexander Young (born 1918)** A World War II veteran and former Ford employee, Young entered Michigan politics as a delegate to the 1961 state constitutional convention and served in the state senate (1964–73), when he became Detroit's first African-American mayor. He served an unprecedented five terms.

**Lee Iacocca (born 1924)**
Child of Italian immigrants, Iacocca joined the Ford Motor Company in 1946 and eventually became its president. After moving to the Chrysler Corporation in 1978, he oversaw the company's recovery from an economic slump.

**Berry Gordy (born 1929)** A Detroit native, Gordy ran a record store and worked for Ford before founding Motown Records. Often showcasing local talent, Motown is one of America's most successful African-American enterprises.

**Lily Tomlin (born 1939)**
This versatile Detroit-born comedian and actress has won awards for work on stage, screen, and on television and records.

**Stevie Wonder (born 1950)**
Born Steveland Judkins Morris in Saginaw, this blind singer and composer signed with Motown Records at the age of ten and had his first hit, *Fingertips*, two years later.

**Pictures in this volume:**

Amy Suhay: 33

Dover: 9, 31, 32

Ford Library: 45

Ford Corporation: 34, 51 (bottom)

Franklin D. Roosevelt Library: 39 (bottom)

George Meany Memorial Archives: 40

Henry Ford Museum and Greenfield Village: 35, 36 (both)

Library of Congress: 8, 10, 12 (both), 13, 15, 16, 19, 21, 22, 23, 24, 25, 27, 28, 30, 43, 47, 48 (bottom), 52

Michigan Travel Authority: 53

MPI Archives: 7, 11, 14, 18, 39 (top), 42, 46, 48 (top), 51 (top)

Museum of the City of New York: 20

National Archives: 29, 37, 41

**About the author:**
Charles A. Wills is a writer, editor, and consultant specializing in American history. He has written, edited, or contributed to more than thirty books, including many volumes in The Millbrook Press's *American Albums from the Collections of the Library of Congress* series. Wills lives in Dutchess County, New York.

**Suggested reading:**

Fradin, Dennis B., *Michigan In Words and Pictures,* Chicago: Children's Press, 1980

Gringhuis, Dirk, *The Great Parade: Tall Tales and True Stories of Michigan's Past,* Hillsdale, MI: Hillsdale Educational Publishers, 1970

Riegle, Marge M., *Wonderland of Michigan,* Fenton, MI: McRoberts, 1981

Simonds, Christopher, *The Model T Ford,* Englewood Cliffs, NJ: Silver Burdett, 1991

Thompson, Kathleen, *Michigan,* Austin, TX: Raintree Steck-Vaughn Publishers, 1996

Wermuth, Mary L, *Images of Michigan: A History*, Hillsdale, MI: Hillsdale Educational Publishers, 1981.

**For more information contact:**

Michigan Travel Bureau
P.O. Box 3393
Livonia, MI 48151-3393
(800)543-2937

Michigan Department of State
History Division, State Archives Unit
3405 North Logan Street
Lansing, MI 48918
(517)373-0512

# INDEX

**Page numbers in *italics* indicate illustrations**